FAIRYTALES FROM HISTORIC FLORIDA
Christmas in El Jardin

Written and Illustrated by
Alejandra Bunster-Elsesser

*"If you want your children to be intelligent read them fairytales.
If you want them to be very intelligent, read them more fairytales."* – Albert Einstein

I dedicate this book to:

El Jardin, home to dear Carrollton School of The Sacred Heart,
where I have been able to work on Creative Expression
with students of all ages and the educators who understand how
essential creativity is in education.

This book was originally created as a gift for Suzanne Cooke, RSCJ,
Carrollton's Headmistress from 1998-2015, to celebrate the school's 50th anniversary.
Just like this story's protagonist, Sister Cooke's mother's name was Irene.
She too dressed very elegantly and loved books.

To Irène Delaroière, House of Arts, Paris.

I am glad to present *Christmas in El Jardin*, in the year *El Jardin* celebrates its 100th birthday.
Happy Centennial Anniversary, beautiful *El Jardin!* And many more!

Contents

Christmas in *El Jardin*..1

Educational Facts on South Florida's History and Nature........................48

Creative Expression *El Jardin's* Alphabet..56

Copyright © 2018 Library of Congress
All rights reserved.

Summary: Irene is a unique ladybug who dresses elegantly, loves to read, and is especially fond of books. With the help of her friends, she will give a very special gift to *El Jardin* who is celebrating its Centennial Anniversary.
ISBN: 978-0-692-19115-6

www.fairytalesfromhistoricflorida.com

The month of December is about to begin, and the entire school is inspired! Everyone is preparing gifts.

Irene will give the school a very special one.

Irene is a unique
ladybug
that brings
good fortune,
as all lady bugs do.

She dresses elegantly,
loves to read,
and is especially
fond of
books.

She was born in a small forest of linden trees in the gardens of the *Hotel Biron* (presently the *Rodin Museum* in Paris), which once housed a notable school.

She traveled from Paris to Coconut Grove, Florida between two pages of the fairytale *Donkey skin* written by Charles Perrault.
He is one of Irene's favorite French authors.

He also wrote *Cinderella, Sleeping Beauty, Little Red Riding Hood*, and many other fairytales that you might have read.

Irene loves the arts:
dance, music,
theater, painting,
drawing, writing,
design, photography,
architecture,
and all forms of
artistic expression.

She believes that
the arts nourish the soul.

Her dream was to come to America.

So, one morning, after carefully packing her most precious belongings - including her amazing collection of umbrellas in many colors and styles - she walked to the nearest post office and got inside a shipment of books.

It was addressed to a school's headmistress, whose office was in *El Jardin*.

Irene now lives in *El Jardin,* a magnificent house built in 1918 surrounded by nature in front of the Bay.

Today, *El Jardin* is home to a wonderful school for girls.

In the *Oak Library*, on top of the bookshelf closest
to the window facing Biscayne Bay,
is her little bedroom.

She decorated it beautifully, using refined papers,
delicate fabrics, colorful yarn, and other materials
she found in different classrooms.
She designed a warm quilt, embroidered with a
unicorn, to cover her tiny acorn for a bed.

Every morning when she wakes up,
before getting out of bed,
Irene closes her eyes in gratitude.

It is always great to start the day
thankfully.

She stays in

and feels the love in her heart.

Irene is very sociable and enjoys the company of her three closest friends: Isabella Peacock, Cardinalis-Cardinalis, and Cathay.

The three of them also live in historic landmarks in front of Biscayne Bay.
All these historical houses are sanctuaries to some of the last remaining hardwood hammocks in Miami, home to exquisite native flora and fauna.

Isabella Peacock, a beautiful peahen, is an event designer and creates all kinds of wonderful celebrations.

She lives at *The Barnacle*, the oldest house in Coconut Grove.

Cardinalis-Cardinalis is a magnificent red bird
who visits the school around Christmas time.
When he is in Miami, he lives at the *Charles Deering Estate.*
When he is not, he lives in Paris where he studies design.

Cathay, an Eastern Tiger Swallowtail butterfly, is a storyteller. She loves film, English, and Chinoiseries. She lives at *Vizcaya Museum and Gardens*, in the Cathay Bedroom, which is decorated in the Chinoiserie style, of course.

The four of them love *to listen and to observe.*

They often fly through *El Jardin's Fairy Garden* towards the water to marvel at the colors of the sunrise and enjoy the breeze on their faces coming from Biscayne Bay.

They observe the clouds that constantly move creating different forms and guess what they are.

They admire the various designs of trees, flowers, and all that surrounds them.

They close their eyes and recognize other birds by their songs.

From the blue jays to the cardinals, from the egrets to the herons, and from the woodpeckers to the hummingbirds.

During assembly in
El Jardin's large courtyard,
they observe the
students' faces
looking attentively at their
loving teachers
and school director,
who on special occasions,
plays the violin.

Today is a
very special occasion.
Everyone is preparing gifts
to celebrate
El Jardin's
Centennial Anniversary!

El Jardin will be 100 years old!

Irene asks her friends to help her with ideas for her gift. They often collaborate on artistic projects.

She invites them for tea over the weekend when all is quiet. She prepares a fire in the *Oak Library's* charming chimney and the room feels cozy and warm. They all start to look for ideas and find inspiration in nature, images, quotes, and books.

So many ideas start to emerge!

Cathay suggests covering the gardens with Cherokee roses that will perfume the air with their sweet clove-like fragrance.

Isabella offers
to bring a
symphony orchestra,
made up of
colorful
hummingbirds,
to perform
in the
Fairy Garden
under the stars.

Cardinalis –Cardinalis reminds them that it is the month of December and Christmas is coming.

He proposes decorating *El Jardin* with thousands and thousands of red birds.

For that, he would call all the cardinals from Miami to Key West to fly to *El Jardin*, and together they would create a spectacular design.

Irene loves all these ideas!

Suddenly, an inspired Irene invites them to fly with her to the *Everglades*. They bring back the most beautiful Florida Pine wrapped in a long golden yarn. They transplant it into a big clay pot and place it in *El Jardin's* courtyard.

The gift will be:

The 12 Christmas Ornaments that bring Eternal Good Fortune.

Each ornament is a symbol for a different wish.

Inspired by some of her favorite books, stories, and characters, Irene makes the ornaments herself.

A House for Protection

Madeline is a book series, written and illustrated by Ludwig Bemelmans. It was first published in 1939. "In an old house in Paris that was covered with vines, lived twelve little girls...the smallest one was Madeline."

A Bird for Joy

"Joy is the most heavenly atmosphere found on Earth."
— Janet Erskine Stuart RSCJ.

The Nightingale is a literary fairy tale written by Danish author Hans Christian Andersen about an emperor who prefers the chant of an ornamented mechanical bird to the song of a real nightingale.

A Fish for *Blessings*

The Tale of the Fisherman and the Fish is a folk-tale about a fisherman who manages to catch a *Golden Fish* which promises to fulfill any wish of his in exchange for its freedom.

A Fruit basket for Generosity

Handa's Surprise, written by Eileen Browne,
is a delightful story of a little girl called Handa who takes a
fruit basket to her friend Akeyo in Kenya.

A Flower basket for Good Wishes

Little Red Riding Hood, written by Charles Perrault,
is a fairy tale about a
young girl and a big bad wolf.

A Heart for love

Feast day of Saint Valentine;
the celebration of love and affection.

A Teapot for *Hospitality*

Alice's Adventures in Wonderland is an 1865 novel written by English author Lewis Carroll.

A Pine Cone for *Fruitfulness*

Elsa Beskow was a Swedish author and illustrator of children's books. Among her better known books are *Tale of the Little Little Old Woman* and *Aunt Green, Aunt Brown and Aunt Lavender*.

A Rabbit for *Hope*

First published in 1902, *The Tale of Peter Rabbit*
is the original classic by
author and illustrator Beatrix Potter.

A Rose for *Beauty*

John Bindley, El Jardin's owner, built Cherokee Lodge across
the street from El Jardin for his sister Mary McMillin.
It was named after the Cherokee roses
that once grew abundantly on the property.

Saint Nicholas for *Goodwill*

Also known as Santa Claus,
Kris Kringle,
Father Christmas,
or simply Santa.

An Angel for
God's Guidance

On that very night, when the entire school
traditionally gathers to sing Christmas carols,
Irene and her friends present the gift.

The ornaments hang gracefully on the
Florida Pine Christmas tree.
What a delightful surprise! Everyone loves the gift!
They all joyfully sing!

Happy Centennial Anniversary,
dear El Jardin.

When all the guests have gone,
Irene, Isabella, Cardinalis-Cardinalis, and Cathay
thankfully sit in *El Jardin's* back garden
reciting the famous poem engraved near the pool:

*"The kiss of the sun for pardon,
the song of the birds for mirth.
One is nearer God's heart in a garden,
than anywhere else on earth."*

The End

HISTORICAL FACTS ON SOUTH FLORIDA'S HISTORY AND NATURE

El Jardin, Coconut Grove, Florida

Built in 1918   Added to the National Register of Historic Places in 1974

El Jardin is home to Carrollton School of the Sacred Heart. The Society of the Sacred Heart purchased the estate in 1961. The beautiful campus has inspired generations of young women to lead and to serve with courage and confidence.

El Jardin was among several grand estates developed along the shores of Biscayne Bay during early twentieth century. Pittsburgh Steel President John Bindley built the home in 1918 as a winter retreat for his daughter Adelaide Marie Bindley. The estate was designed by noted architects Kiehnel & Elliot and is one of the earliest and best-preserved examples of Mediterranean-Revival architecture in South Florida.

"Spanish, Italian, Moorish, Byzantine...are under this orchestrated process merged...into a sun-loving style which, while eminently American in its plan and utilities, is nevertheless distinctly Mediterranean in its origins and spirit". - Rexford Newcomb

THE TWELVE CHRISTMAS ORNAMENTS THAT BRING ETERNAL GOOD FORTUNE.

According to an old German tradition, a couple's Christmas tree should include twelve symbolic ornaments to ensure happiness in their life journey together.

1. Angel: God's Guidance
2. Flower basket: Good wishes
3. Bird: Joy
4. Heart: Love
5. House: Protection
6. Teapot: Hospitality
7. Saint Nicolas: Goodwill
8. Pine Cone: Fruitfulness
9. Fruit basket: Generosity
10. Rose: Beauty
11. Rabbit: Hope
12. Fish: Blessings

HOTEL BIRON, PARIS, FRANCE

Home to Couvent du Sacré-Coeur, from 1820 to 1905.
Hotel Biron has housed the Musée Auguste Rodin since 1919.

Hotel Biron is located on the rue de Varenne, in Paris' 7th district. It was built from 1727 to 1731 and was designed by the architect to the King, Jean Aubert.

In 1820 the Duchess of Charost sold the entire property to "*La Société du Sacré-Coeur de Jesus*", whose *Dames du Sacré-Coeur*, were dedicated to the education of young women and converted the *Hotel Biron* into a boarding school.

Saint Madeleine Sophie Barat, the founder of the Society, lived there until she passed away in 1865. Under the 1905 French law on the separation of Church and State, however, the school was forced to close.

The original seal of the Society of the Sacred Heart, can still be seen in the Hotel Biron Chapel window.

THE BARNACLE, COCONUT GROVE, FLORIDA
Historic State Park   Built in 1891
The Barnacle is the *oldest* residence in Miami-Dade County remaining on its original foundation.

Commodore Ralph Middleton Munroe, one of the founders of Coconut Grove, purchased 40 acres of bay front land in 1886. His boathouse was built in 1887 and the upper floor served as his home until *The Barnacle*, "the most ingenious and sophisticated work of vernacular architecture remaining from the pioneer days of South Florida was built. The design reflects Munroe's knowledge of boat building and naval architecture."

As you walk into this site you are surrounded by a forest called a tropical Hardwood Hammock that still exists thanks to Ralph Munroe's love of nature. The forest contains many old trees and appears much as it did in Munroe's day.

Cocoanut Grove (as it was called) was the first community on the South Florida mainland.

VIZCAYA MUSEUM AND GARDENS
Founded in 1916   National Historic Landmark

Vizcaya is the former villa and winter estate home of businessman James Deering, of the Deering McCormick-International Harvester fortune and is located on Biscayne Bay in Miami, Florida.

It was designed in the style of the Italian Renaissance and Baroque villas that Deering had visited, and adapted to the subtropical climate of South Florida.

F. Burrall Hoffman (1882-1980) designed the buildings. Diego Suarez (1888-1974) planned the gardens and Paul Chalfin (1873-1959) was the general artistic director.

In 1917 John Singer visited *Vizcaya* and created watercolors of the estate.

CHARLES DEERING ESTATE
National Register of Historic Places   Built in 1922

Home of Charles Deering, brother of James Deering, owner of *Vizcaya*, was an American businessman, and a philanthropist. Deering acquired the 444 acre property in 1914.

The property consists of:
Richmond House, 1896: a small two-story frame vernacular building, home of the pioneer Richmond family.
Richmond Cottage, 1900: a three floor wooden house, known as the Richmond Inn, the first Inn between Coconut Grove and Key West.
Stone House, 1922: an impressive Mediterranean Revival style structure, safe repository for his valuable art and antique collection.

The first road from Coconut Grove, built in 1882, runs through the property and serves now as the park's main hammock trail, where native plant species like oak, gumbo limbo, pigeon plum and an abundance of wild butterflies can be found.

One of the most significant features in the property, dating from 1500-1700, is a Tequesta Burial Mound. Artifacts from the mound are from the Glades II and III periods.

PEAHENS AND PEACOCKS

The male is called a peacock, best known for the extravagant eye-spotted tail covered feathers, which it displays as part of courtship. The female is called a peahen and the offspring peachicks.

Our Isabella's last name: Peacock, is a family name that belongs to the early settlers in Coconut Grove. Charles and Isabella Peacock emigrated from England in 1870. They opened *the Bay View House* in 1882, the first hotel on Biscayne Bay. It was later renamed the *Peacock Inn*. It was torn down in 1926, and later became a park, which was named *Peacock Park* in honor of the Peacocks. Charles and Isabella Peacock had three sons: Henry, Alfred and Charles John. Alfred Peacock married Lillian Frow (daughter of Joseph Frow, assistant to his brother John, the Cape Florida Lighthouse keeper); their daughter Eunice Isabella Peacock later married George Merrick, the founder of Coral Gables.

LADY BUGS, (*Coccinellidae*)

Derived from the Latin word *coccineus* meaning "scarlet".

The name "Ladybird" originated in Britain where the insects became known as "Our Lady's bird" or "Lady beetle". Mary (named "Our Lady" in reference to the mother of Jesus Christ) was often depicted wearing a red cloak in early paintings, and the spots of the seven-spot Ladybird (the most common in Europe) were said to symbolize her seven joys and seven sorrows.

In the United States, the name was adapted to "Ladybug". When entomologists need to use a common name, they widely prefer the names "Lady Bird beetles" or "Lady beetles" as *these insects are not true bugs.*

FLORIDA PINE, (Pinus Elliottii), OR SLASH PINE

Much of South Florida was once covered by a vast expanse of forestland. It gave South Florida a tropical accent found nowhere else in the continental United States.

South Florida Pine, also known as "Dade County Pine" was used widely in the construction of many historic buildings in the Miami and Key West areas. At the present rate of decline, it is possible that all our pine and hammock forestland outside of Everglades National Park could disappear before the year 2020.

Coral Gables was originally called "Among the Pines".

Christmas card by Ms. Merrick

EL JARDIN translates from Spanish to THE GARDEN

The verse engraved on top of the swimming pool area at *El Jardin*:

"The kiss of the sun for pardon, the song of the birds for mirth, One is nearer God's heart in a garden, than anywhere else on earth" ...

inspired *the Society of the Sacred Heart* to purchase the beautiful property where El Jardin stands in front of the Bay.

God's Garden

"THE Lord God planted a garden
In the first white days of the world,
And He set there an angel warden
In a garment of light unfurled.
So near to the peace of Heaven,
That the hawk might nest with the wren,
For there in the cool of the even
God walked with the first of men.
And I dream that these garden-closes
With their shade and their sun-flecked sod
And their lilies and bowers of roses,
Were laid by the hand of God.
*The kiss of the sun for pardon,
the song of the birds for mirth,
One is nearer God's heart in a garden,
than anywhere else on earth.*
For He broke it for us in a garden
Under the olive-trees
Where the angel of strength was the warden
And the soul of the world found ease."

- Dorothy Frances Gurney
English poet and hymn writer.

The cultivation of expressive and creative potential is essential in the formation of every human being and beneficial to all ages and walks of life.

El Jardin's Alphabet

Acorn Books Classroom Desk El Jardin

Fruits Garden Hummingbird Irene Jam

Kitchen Love Music Noise Oak tree

Pencils Quilt Rain Silence Teacher

Umbrella Violin Water Xylophone Yarn

Zzzzzzzzzz

"Creativity lives in paradox: serious art is born from serious play." – Julia Cameron

EL JARDIN'S ALPHABET

Exercise to cultivate Creativity and Imagination

Acorn · Books · Classroom · Desk · El Jardin · Fruits · Garden · Hummingbird · Irene · Jam · Kitchen · Love · Music · Noise · Oak tree · Pencils · Quilt · Rain · Silence · Teacher · Umbrella · Violin · Water · Xylophone · Yarn · Zzzzzzzzz

WRITE STORIES

INSTRUCTIONS:

Using the first three letters of your name, create a story with words from EL JARDIN'S ALPHABET.

Example: Your name: Margaret.   M=Music   A=Acorn   R=Rain

Once upon a time there was a beautiful girl named Margaret, she was a musician who had a vivid imagination. On rainy days she imagined the raindrops as musical notes falling down from the sky in the shape of tiny colored acorns.
One day...

Can you finish this story?

Can you give the story three different endings?

Would you like to Illustrate it?

Example written on the spot, by Cecilia Swain, 8th grade student.

Caro (for Carolina):

Classroom, Acorn, Rain, Oaktree

Walking into my first English class of the year, my classmates and I got seated in the U-shaped desk layout in the *classroom*. Our new English teacher, Mrs. Scott, told us our first classwork assignment was to write about our Fourth of July and what was special about it.

"Caro," she had said after we had finished writing, "Please read to us about your Fourth of July." I slowly rose from my chair, and eagerly started sharing my story.

"My Fourth of July started out on the beach, where my family and I swam and hung out, and for lunch, my dad made burgers for my mother, sister and me. While he was at the public grill, my sister and I were sitting at a picnic table next to an *oak tree*. There were a lot of squirrels on that tree, around five of them, and they went nuts for some reason. They started to throw *acorns* at us! I will always remember that this Fourth of July, it was *raining* acorns."

NOW TRY IT USING:

- All the letters in your mother's name.
- All the letters in your father's name.
- Your best friend's name.
- Select five letters of your choice.
- You can create many different stories with the same letters.
- Come up with your own way of playing this game!

QUESTIONS:

- Which of the words from El Jardin's Alphabet are used in the story *Christmas in El Jardin*?
- Which words are not used in the story?
- Can you write a story with all the words from El Jardin's Alphabet?
- What would be your gift to *El Jardin*?

CREATE YOUR OWN EL JARDIN'S ALPHABET

Use other words for each letter in the alphabet.

Illustrate each word and create a card game.

You can use the same instructions above, or create your own.

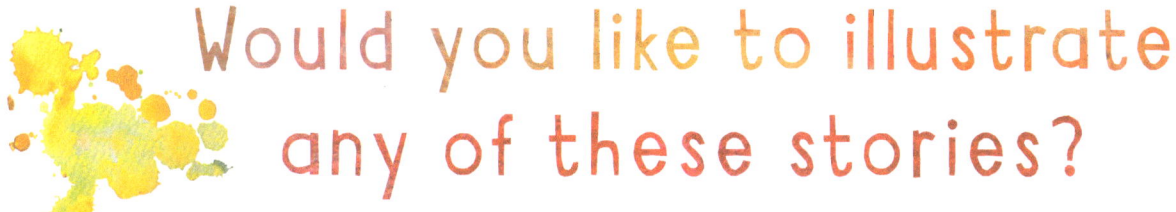

Would you like to illustrate any of these stories?

My eternal gratitude to those who inspired, helped or supported the making of this book and the *Fairytales From Historic Florida* series.

Here are their favorite children's books:

MAX BUNSTER: *Peter Pan* by J. M. Barrie.
MAX G BUNSTER: *Curious George* by Margaret and H. A. Rey.
ALASTAIR BUNSTER: *The Giving Tree* by Shel Silverstein.
POLA BUNSTER: *Peter the Rabbit* by Beatrix Potter, *Madeline* by Ludwig Bemelmans, *The Phantom Tollbooth* by Norton Juster, illustrations by Jules Feiffer.

Carrollton School of the Sacred Heart

ANN TAYLOR, RSCJ, Carolllton's Headmistress 1978-1998:
For the very young *Make Way for Ducklings* written and illustrated by Robert McCloskey, a little older: *Black Beauty* by Anna Sewell, and a little older: *Grimm's Fairytales.*
SUZANNE COOKE, RSCJ, Carrollton's Headmistress 1998-2015:
Babar the Elephant, Histoire de Babar by Jean de Brunhoff.
OLEN KALKUS, Head Master 2015-present: My recent: *Horton Hears a Who!* by Dr. Seuss.
Favorite children's Christmas book: *The Christmas Carp* by Rita and Marit Tornqvist.
PAOLA CONSUEGRA, Director of Montessori & Primary School: *The Giving Tree* by Shel Silverstein.
HEATHER GILLINGHAM, Director of the Intermediate School: *Panda Cake* by Rosalie Seidler.
LOURDES WOOD, Director of the Junior High School: *The Giving Tree* by Shel Silverstein.
DENISE ORTEGA, Director of Institutional Advancement: *The Little Prince* by Antoine de Saint-Exupéry.
IRIS GUZMAN KOLAYA '96, mother of Alexandra '27 and Sienna Kolaya '29:
Goodnight Moon by Margaret Wise Brown, illustrated by Clement Hurd.
MELINEE FERNANDEZ, Director of Information Service: *Charlotte's Web* by E.B. White, illustrated by Garth Williams.
ROBBIE RAND, Librarian: *The Giving Tree* by Shel Silverstein.
KIM KALKUS, Library clerk: Anything by Dame Lynley Dodd, *HairyMaclary* series.
SHAUNE SCOTT, 8th Grade English teacher: *Little Women* by Louisa May Alcott.
CECILIA SWAIN, 8th Grade student (representing all students who have attended Creative Expression courses): *The Little Prince* by Antoine de Saint-Exupéry.
KARI SNYDER, Graphic designer: *May the Stars Drip Down* by Jeremy Chatelain, illustrated by Nikki McClure.

MITCHELL KAPLAN, 2011 recipient of The National Book Foundation Lifetime Achievement Award, owner of Books & Books, co-founder of the Miami Book Fair International, and Film Producer: *The Red Balloon* by Albert Lamorisse.

www.ingramcontent.com/pod-product-compliance
Lightning Source LLC
Chambersburg PA
CBHW042147290426
44110CB00003B/137